world tour
Germany

CHRISTOPHER MITTEN

Raintree

www.raintreepublishers.co.uk
Visit our website to find out more information about Raintree books.

To order:
☎ Phone 44 (0) 1865 888112
▯ Send a fax to 44 (0) 1865 314091
▯ Visit the Raintree Bookshop at www.raintreepublishers.co.uk to browse our catalogue and order online.

First published in Great Britain by Raintree Publishers, Halley Court, Jordan Hill, Oxford, OX2 8EJ, part of Harcourt Education.
Raintree is a registered trademark of Harcourt Education Ltd.

© Harcourt Education Ltd 2003
First published in paperback 2004
The moral right of the proprieter has been asserted.

Editorial: Sally Knowles
Cover Design: Peter Bailey and Michelle Lisseter
Production: Jonathan Smith

Printed and bound in China and Hong Kong by South China Printing Company

ISBN 1 44 21312 9 (hardback)
07 06 05 04 03
10 9 8 7 6 5 4 3 2 1

ISBN 1 844 21326 9 (paperback)
08 07 06 05 04
10 9 8 7 6 5 4 3 2 1

British Library Cataloguing in Publication Data
Mitten, Christopher
Germany. - (World tour)
943
A full catalogue for this book is available from the British Library

Acknowledgements
The publishers would like to thank the following for permission to reproduce photographs:
p. **1a** ©Bob Krist/CORBIS; p. **1b** ©Steve Vidler/eStock; p. **3a** ©Steve Vidler/eStock; p. **3b** ©Bob Krist/CORBIS; p. **5** ©H. Armstrong Roberts; p. **6** ©Kevin Galvin; p. **7** ©Elsen/Mauritius/H. Armstrong Roberts; p. **8** ©Alan Kaye/ DRK; p. **13** ©Bob Krist/CORBIS; p. **14** ©Franz-Marc Frei/CORBIS; p. **15** ©Kevin Galvin; p. **16** ©Viesti Associates, Inc.; p. **19** ©Reuters NewMedia Inc./CORBIS; p. **21a** ©Photo Library International, Ltd./eStock; p. **21b** ©Pictor/Uniphoto; p. **25a** ©Reuters NewMedia, Inc/CORBIS; p. **25b** Kevin Galvin; p. **26** ©Peter Harnholdt/CORBIS; p. **27** ©Christopher Cormack/CORBIS; p. **28** ©Owen Franken/CORBIS; p. **29** ©AFP/CORBIS; p. **31a** ©Dr Lorenz/H. Armstrong Roberts; p. **31b** ©Kevin Galvin; p. **33** ©Dallas and John Heaton/ CORBIS; p. **34** © Dennis Gottlieb/FoodPix; p. **35** ©Bill Boch/FoodPix; p. **37a** ©Bob Krist/CORBIS; p. **37b** ©Tom Nebbia/CORBIS; p. **39a** ©Kevin Galvin; p. **39b** ©Pat Armstrong/Visuals Unlimited; p. **40** ©AFP/CORBIS; p. **41** Owen Franken/CORBIS; p. **42** ©Viesti Associates, Inc.; p. **43b** ©Bob Krist/CORBIS; p. **43c** ©European Central Bank, Frankfurt; p. **44a, b** ©Hulton Archive; p. **44c** ©Mitchell Gerber/CORBIS.

Additional photography by Getty Images Royalty Free and Steck-Vaughn Collection.

Cover photography: Background: Powerstock/Bruno Morandi. Foreground: Pictures Colour Library

Every effort has been made to contact copyright holders of any material reproduced in this book. Any omissions will be rectified in subsequent printing if notice is given to the publishers.

Contents

Welcome to Germany

Germany is a fascinating and dynamic country and an exciting place to visit. In Germany you can explore **enchanted** forests and ancient castles. You can visit quiet villages and modern cities. This book introduces you to the country and its history.

Some tips to get you started

• Use the table of contents

Do you already know what you are looking for? Perhaps you just want to know what topics this book covers. The contents page tells you what you can read about. It tells you where to find them in the book.

• Look at the pictures

This book has lots of great photos. Flip through and look at the pictures you like best. They will show you what the book is all about. Read the captions to learn more about the photos.

• Use the glossary

As you read this book, you may notice that some words appear in **bold** print. Look up bold words in the glossary at the back of the book. The glossary will help you learn what they mean.

▲ PLEASURE DRIVE
This world-famous motorway network, the Autobahn, is more than 11,000 km (6800 miles) long. A top speed of 130 km/hr (about 80 mph) is recommended but is not law.

Germany's past

Before you start your tour, explore Germany's past. To understand Germany today, it helps to know its history.

Ancient history

The first Germans began to settle in the area about 5500 years ago. Around 100 BC, several German tribes came into contact with the Romans. In AD 9, the Romans attacked the German settlers but were defeated in the Battle of the Teutoburg Forest.

Age of kings

Over the years, many different kings ruled Germany. Around 500, Germany was linked to France by a king called Clovis who came from a tribe called the Franks. He was important because he became a Christian and helped spread Christianity in Germany.

In the 730s, a dynasty called the Carolingians came to power. Charlemagne was most famous Carolingian king. In 843, his kingdom was divided up among his grandsons. For the next 1000 years, Germany was divided into lots of small kingdoms.

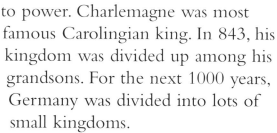

◀ **GARGOYLES**
Gargoyles were used long ago to ward off evil spirits. In Germany, you will find gargoyles on many buildings.

The **Reformation** was one of
the most important events in
European history and it began
in Germany. During the
Reformation, the Protestant
church was **founded** by
Martin Luther. In 1517, he nailed a paper to the door of
the main church in Wittenberg. It contained 95 ideas he
had about Christianity. Most of his ideas criticized the
Roman Catholic church. Luther's ideas are now called
'The 95 Theses'. For 100 years after Luther's death,
Catholics and Protestants fought all over Germany until
1648, when they declared a **truce** called the Peace
of Westphalia.

Formation of a nation

After the Reformation, most of the land that is now
Germany was called Prussia. In 1871 Prussia was
unified as Germany by Otto Von Bismarck who was
chancellor under King Wilhelm I. In 1871, the king
was renamed the Kaiser, or Emperor, of Germany.
Bismarck became known as the Iron Chancellor.

▲ **THE HOLOCAUST REMEMBERED**
This is the site of a German concentration camp at Dachau.
The sign is pointing to the shelters (bunker) and the
crematoriums (krematorium). Millions of Jews died in Nazi
camps during the Holocaust.

World wars and the Holocaust

The new Germany grew very powerful over the next
40 years, alarming many other European countries.
In 1914, World War I began and lasted until Germany
was defeated in 1918.

By 1929, Germany was in trouble because of a
worldwide **economic depression**. In 1934, the

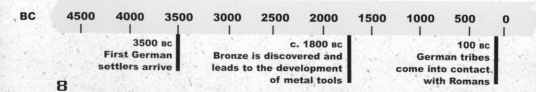

BC	4500	4000	3500	3000	2500	2000	1500	1000	500	0

3500 BC
First German
settlers arrive

c. 1800 BC
Bronze is discovered and
leads to the development
of metal tools

100 BC
German tribes
come into contact
with Romans

National Socialist Party – the **Nazi party** – took over, led by Adolf Hitler. He blamed Germany's problems on other European countries and on the Jews. In 1939, Britain, France and Russia declared war on Germany after Hitler **invaded** Poland. For the next six years, most of the world was at war.

During World War II, the Nazis committed a horrible crime. They rounded up Jewish people and sent them to **death camps**. More than 6 million Jewish men, women and children were murdered in the camps. This terrible period in history is called the **Holocaust**.

Germany divided, Germany reunified

After the war, Germany was divided in two. Germany's capital, Berlin, was also divided. East Germany and East Berlin were **Communist**. In 1961, the Communists built a wall through the centre of the city called the Berlin Wall.

Germany remained divided for 38 years. This period is often considered part of the **cold war**. The cold war came to an end when the Soviet Union collapsed. In 1989 the Berlin Wall was torn down. In 1990, East and West Germany were finally reunited.

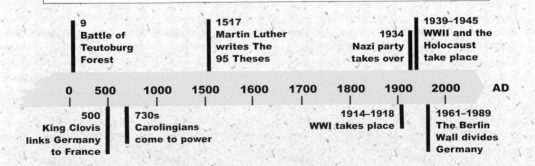

9
Battle of
Teutoburg
Forest

1517
Martin Luther
writes The
95 Theses

1934
Nazi party
takes over

1939–1945
WWII and the
Holocaust
take place

0 500 1000 1500 1600 1700 1800 1900 2000 AD

500
King Clovis
links Germany
to France

730s
Carolingians
come to power

1914–1918
WWI takes place

1961–1989
The Berlin
Wall divides
Germany

A look at Germany's geography

Germany is famous for its beautiful landscapes. It is a country with beautiful valleys, snow-capped mountains and rushing rivers. This makes Germany a perfect place for visitors to explore.

The land

Germany is part of Central Europe. In the south of the country are Germany's highest mountains, the Bavarian Alps. The highest peak in the Bavarian Alps is called Zugspitze and it is 2962 metres tall.

The Jura Mountains of France and Switzerland continue into southern Germany, where they are called the Swabian Jura. The Swabian Jura are not as tall as the Bavarian Alps – the highest peak is the Lemberg at 1015 metres. The mountains overlap with Germany's Black Forest, or Schwarzwald. The Schwarzwald got its name from the dark evergreen trees that grow there.

To the north of the Bavarian Alps and the Black Forest lie the central uplands and the Harz Mountains. The highest point in this region is Brocken Peak, which stands at 1136 metres.

The northern region of Germany is a wet, low-lying plain. There are many rivers in this part of Germany and they keep the surrounding soil **fertile** and excellent for farming.

GERMANY'S SIZE ▶

Germany covers 137,828 sq miles (356,973 sq km). To Germany's north is Denmark. To the west lie the Netherlands, Belgium, Luxembourg and France. To the south of Germany are Switzerland and Austria. To Germany's east are the Czech Republic and Poland.

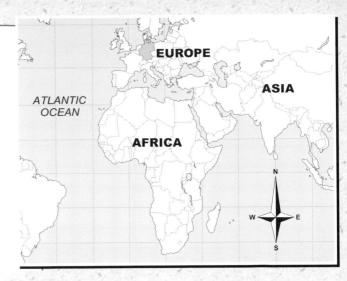

GERMANY

- ★ National capital
- • Major city

```
0      50    100 Kilometres
0      50        100 Miles
```

Water

Germany has coastline on two seas separated by the Jutland Peninsula. To the north-west of the Jutland Peninsula is the North Sea and to the north-east is the Baltic Sea. Germany contains several lakes; the biggest is Bodensee – Lake Constance in English.

Germany has several major rivers. The Danube runs through the southern part of Germany. The Elbe runs from the central uplands through the city of Hamburg, and into the North Sea. In the west lies the Rhine. Each of these rivers flows into other countries. The Rhine provides a natural border between Germany and France.

GERMANY

★ National capital
— River
▲ Mountain

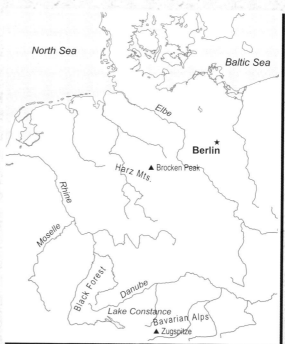

North Sea

Baltic Sea

Elbe

★ Berlin

Harz Mts. ▲ Brocken Peak

Rhine

Moselle

Black Forest

Danube

Lake Constance

Bavarian Alps
▲ Zugspitze

▲ THE RHINE
People have lived along the Rhine for centuries. This ancient castle was built to overlook the river.

◀ FUN IN THE SNOW
In the winter, the snow in the Bavarian Alps is great for toboganning. These thrill-seekers may be getting more than they bargained for.

The weather

Germany has a **temperate** climate which means that it does not get very hot or very cold. The weather varies from region to region. In Hamburg, near the north coast, the temperatures average about 0°C in winter and 17°C at the height of summer. Temperatures in Munich, in the far south of Germany, average about -2°C in the winter and 18°C in the summer. The Bavarian Alps are the coldest and wettest area of Germany.

Overall, the average temperature in Germany during January is around 0°C. During July, the average temperature rises to about 18°C.

▲ **RAINY DAYS**
**Autumn and winter bring cold and rain to Germany. Visitors
should bring coats or umbrellas.**

Berlin: snapshot of a big city

▲ **OVERLOOKING BERLIN**
The city of Berlin has a lot to offer. It is a beautiful city with a fascinating past.

No trip to Germany is complete without a visit to Berlin. Its wide boulevards, ancient buildings and beautiful parks make it ideal for a holiday.

Berlin's past

After World War II, Germany was divided in two parts – East and West Germany. The eastern half had a Communist government like the Soviet Union, while West Germany had a democratic government. Berlin was also divided. In 1961, the communists built a wall through the middle of Berlin so people could not leave East Berlin for the West. In 1989, the people of Berlin tore down the wall.

West Berlin

The best place to start a tour of Berlin is the Tiergarten, which is a huge park. Tiergarten is German for 'animal garden'. It is called this because there is a beautiful zoo in the Tiergarten.

At the east end of the Tiergarten is the Reichstag, the home of the German parliament. The Kurfürstendamm is one of Berlin's best shopping districts. You could also visit the Berlin Museum, which tells the story of Berlin.

East Berlin

When Berlin was divided by the wall, there was a famous gateway between East and West Berlin called Checkpoint Charlie. Nothing remains of the border crossing today. But there is an excellent museum there called Haus am Checkpoint Charlie which explains how and why the Berlin Wall was constructed. It also tells the sad story of the hundreds of people who died while trying to escape East Berlin.

After leaving the museum, there is plenty to explore in the area where the wall once stood. The wall is gone, but its remains are still there. Tourists used to chip little pieces off the wall as souvenirs. Today, the rubble that remains is protected, so no-one can take a piece away.

Next, walk to the Brandenburg Gate. This is one of the most impressive monuments in the whole of Berlin. It was built to celebrate German power.

South of the Berlin Wall are the remains of Hitler's bunker. It was here that he committed suicide when he realized that he had lost the war. Hitler's bunker is now a **memorial** to the destruction and murder caused by the Nazis during World War II and the Holocaust.

Continue east towards Alexanderplatz, one of the most famous squares in Berlin. It was here that East Germans began to protest against the Berlin Wall in 1989. A few days after the demonstrations, the wall was torn down. Alexanderplatz is not Berlin's most beautiful spot, but it is one of the most important. It is where Berlin began its new future.

BERLIN WALL ▶
**A demonstrator helps knock down
the Berlin Wall. Until 1989, it
separated East and West Berlin.**

BERLIN'S TOP-TEN CHECKLIST

If you are heading to Germany, here is a list of the top ten things you have to do.

☐ Visit the Reichstag. See if you can spot a member of parliament.

☐ Go shopping on the Kurfürstendamm. Look at the expensive shops.

☐ Spend the afternoon at the Berlin Museum.

☐ Visit the remains of the Berlin Wall.

☐ Pass to the East where Checkpoint Charlie used to be.

☐ Walk through the Brandenburg Gate.

☐ Visit Hitler's bunker.

☐ Stroll down Unter den Linden, a beautiful street lined with trees. Take some photos of historic buildings.

☐ Walk around Alexanderplatz, one of Berlin's most famous squares.

☐ Head back to the Tiergarten and spend the afternoon at its zoo.

Four top sights in Germany

Germany is a lively country with lots of exciting places to visit. With so much to choose from, it may be hard to know where to start. Here are four suggestions that should be somewhere on a tourist's schedule.

Hamburg's harbour

Hamburg was built on the mouth of the river Elbe, where it opens into the North Sea. The city was founded by Charlemagne in 810 (see the chapter on Germany's history). Today, Hamburg is one of Europe's largest **ports**. About 15,000 ships come in and out of Hamburg each year, carrying everything from washing machines to lemons, and make Hamburg a centre of international trade.

For travellers, all the activity can be interesting to watch but all those ships and the local industry along the river can cause problems with pollution.

The best way to see Hamburg's harbour is to go on a boat tour. The boat will go very close to the biggest ships in the world so you can watch as crates of coffee are carried into Germany while cargoes of tyres sail off towards the North Sea.

Visitors can also wander around the **docks** on foot and go to the fish market. This is a great place to pick up a few live eels, some oysters or any one of dozens of types of fish.

▼ PORT SIDE
All kinds of products travel in and out of Hamburg's bustling port.

LONG JOB ▶
The harbour is the place to see huge ships docked for repairs or being loaded with goods that will be taken all over the world.

▲ **FAIRYTALE CASTLE**
This castle does not have a moat, a fire-breathing dragon or
a fairytale princess. It was built by King Ludwig II of
Germany in the late 1800s.

Neuschwanstein

If you have ever seen Sleeping Beauty's castle at Disneyland then you will have an idea of what the castle at Neuschwanstein looks like. Disney actually based its castles on this incredible building.

The castle was built by the local ruler, King Ludwig II, at the end of the 19th century. It is near Munich, in the Bavarian Alps. The **architecture** was already old-fashioned, but the king wanted to live in a fairytale palace. In fact, the castle was designed by theatre people who built sets for operas.

Sadly, Ludwig died before the castle was finished, so he never got to live in his dream home, but he left behind a truly unique place for travellers to visit. The best time to see it is in the evening – the sunsets seen from Ludwig's castle are breathtaking.

FASCINATING FACT

When King Ludwig II built this castle in the 1800s, he made it very modern. All the lavatories had automatic flushing. There was a hot water system for the kitchens and baths. There was even a heating system.

Oktoberfest

Oktoberfest is probably Germany's most famous festival. It is sixteen days of eating, drinking, singing and dancing and takes place each autumn in the city of Munich in south-east Germany. It starts on a Saturday in September and ends on the first Sunday in October. Millions of tourists come from all over the world to Oktoberfest because it is a wild and exciting celebration of German **culture**.

Oktoberfest started in 1810, when the people of Munich celebrated a royal wedding with events such as horse races. It was repeated the next year, and then the year after that and so on. They no longer hold horse races, but the tradition of Oktoberfest lives on today.

Germans are world-famous **brewers** of beer and the Oktoberfest is probably best known as a celebration of Germany's fine brews. Beer halls in Munich burst with visitors who crowd around long tables during this festival. People often sing German folk-songs, linking arms and swaying in time to the music as they sing. Sometimes they even get up and dance.

The festivities start with a parade with lots of bands and music. There are horses, and people dressed in traditional German clothes. There are fairground rides, like roller coasters and big wheels and stalls serving traditional German cooking. Music bands come from all over the world to play at this festival. People who like to party love Oktoberfest.

▲ **PARADING ABOUT TOWN**
There is lots of music and dancing in the Oktoberfest parade.

TRADITIONAL MUSIC ▶
Young and old alike can enjoy the live music at Oktoberfest.

The Porsche factory and museum

Germany is very famous for the manufacture of fine cars. BMW, Mercedes and Volkswagen are some of the companies that you might have heard of. One of Germany's coolest (and most expensive) cars is the Porsche. This sleek sports car has long been the car of choice for movie stars and royalty. You can find out all about them at the Porsche factory and museum in the town of Stuttgart.

The visit starts by taking the free guided tour through the factory and watching the highly skilled workers carefully assemble each of the cars. You will see why Germans are known around the world for their top-quality cars.

The museum displays Porsches from the past 50 years. They will not let you drive one, but you will be able to take pictures of these beautiful cars.

IN THE FAST LANE ▼
Germany is a great place to drive a fast car like a Porsche. You can drive at up to 130 km/hr (80 mph) along the German motorway, the Autobahn.

▼ NOT YOUR AVERAGE CAR FACTORY
Highly skilled workers take their time creating these Porsches. Each one has to be perfect.

Going to school in Germany

Children in Germany have to go to school for twelve years. After that, they are free to continue with school or leave to get a job. Usually, Germans spend a year in kindergarten and about four years in elementary school.

After that, students go to one of four kinds of schools. The first is called a *gymnasium*, where students study general subjects such as maths, languages and science. The second is called a *hauptschule* or a *realschule*. This is a **vocational school** that trains students for different jobs. At the third type of school, students study general subjects and also get job training. The fourth offers all three courses of study: the general subjects, the *gymnasium* course and the *hauptschule* course.

Students are taught in German, the official language of Germany. German public schools are considered to be some of the best in the world.

◀ **IN A GERMAN CLASSROOM**
Students can pick from a variety of subjects in German schools. They may even choose to train for a specific job.

German sports

Cycling is one of Germany's most popular sports. Germany hosts many international cycle races, and Germans do very well in races in other countries, as well as in the Olympics.

Tennis is also popular in Germany. The German tennis players Boris Becker and Steffi Graf were two of the world's best players. Today, many young people have followed their example and taken up tennis.

The most popular sport in Germany is football. Germany has a large national football league.

OLYMPIC GOLD ▶
Jens Lehmann rode his way to a gold medal in the 2000 Olympic Games in Sydney, Australia. This was a big win for the country that helped invent bicycles.

From farming to factories

Germany is the third-largest car maker in the world, behind the USA and Japan. The German car industry brings in many euros – which is the type of money used in Germany. Mercedes, Volkswagen and Porsche are a few of these companies. They employ people to design the cars, build them and then sell them all over the world.

German companies also manufacture numerous other products, including plastics, electronics, textiles and chemicals. The high quality of German products is recognized around the world. One reason German products are so good is because Germany has a very good education system. Before a German person goes to work in a factory, he or she has probably learnt many parts of the job in school. Generally, German factories produce goods that are difficult to make – they require a **skilled workforce**.

Some Germans are farmers. They grow grains like oats, wheat and rye as well as vegetables, fruit and sugar beet for sugar. Many raise animals, such as sheep, pigs and cows. Germans use these goods to make food products like bread, sausages and beer.

Other Germans work as doctors, teachers, lawyers, bus drivers and hairdressers – all the sorts of jobs that are needed in any society.

▲ BREWING BEER
Germans are known for enjoying many kinds of
beer. Making the perfect brew is an art that
takes patience and skill.

◄ SHEARING SHEEP
German farmers
shear their sheep for
wool. This wool is
used around the
world to make
jumpers and other
warm clothing.

The German government

The kind of government Germany has today is fairly recent — it started when East and West Germany were reunified in 1990. Germany is now a **democracy**. To become a leader here, a person must win an election.

Germany has two branches of federal government: the parliament, which makes the laws, and the executive, which carries them out. The parliament is divided into two parts: the Bundestag and the Bundesrat. The Bundestag is the more powerful section. It makes the laws for the whole country. The Bundesrat represents the different regions of Germany. Its members make laws that affect their home states — in matters like education or health care.

The chancellor is head of the executive branch of government and is chosen by the Bundestag. He or she is the most powerful person in the government.

GERMANY'S NATIONAL FLAG

The German flag has three bands of colour. The top band is black, the middle is red and the bottom is gold. This flag represents the reunification of East and West Germany.

Religions of Germany

Sixty-eight per cent of Germans are Christians. They follow the teachings of Jesus, as written in the New Testament of the Bible. About half of Germany's Christians are Roman Catholic. Catholics are Christians who also follow the leadership of the Pope, a religious figure who lives near Rome. The other half of German Christians are Protestant, which means that they do not follow the Pope.

Muslims make up 3.7 per cent of the population. Muslims follow the teachings of Mohammed, written in a holy book called the Koran.

About 70,000 Jews live in Germany. They follow the teachings in the Torah, or Old Testament of the Bible.

▲ HISTORIC CHURCHES
These magnificent buildings show the same love of detail as some of Germany's castles.

German food

After a long walk through the Black Forest, or a day of sailing on the North Sea, there is nothing better than sitting down to a meal at a German table. German food is hearty and filling so it is perfect after an active day.

A typical main dish at a German lunch or dinner will be pork, beef, veal or chicken. The meat is served with an elaborate sauce. Side dishes usually include potatoes, bread and vegetables – such as carrots, beetroot or cabbage.

Lighter meals may feature cheeses and preserved meats, sausage, ham and pickled fish. At these meals, Germans eat lots of bread. If you visit Germany, be sure to try as many different kinds of bread as possible. Every one of them is delicious.

Breakfast in Germany is often coffee and pastries. Sometimes it includes cheese and cold sausage. If you are in the north, you might even get a piece of fish for your breakfast.

◀ **DINNER IN GERMANY**
This hearty plate of food is a traditional German meal. Knockwurst is a type of sausage.

Germany's recipe

KARTOFFELPUFFER (POTATO PANCAKES)

INGREDIENTS:

9 medium raw potatoes
1 medium onion, chopped
3 eggs
1 tsp salt
Pinch of pepper
6 tbsp flour
2 tbsp parsley
3 tbsp vegetable oil

WARNING:

**Never cook or bake by yourself.
Always ask an adult to help you in
the kitchen.**

DIRECTIONS:

**Peel and grate the potatoes. Drain the juice from the
potatoes, then mix them with the onion, eggs, salt, pepper,
flour and parsley. Heat the oil in a pan on medium heat. Put
the mixture in the pan 3 tablespoons at a time. Flatten the
pancakes as they cook. Cook until they are golden brown on
both sides.**

Up close: the Black Forest

Lots of people first hear about Germany through folk-tales, such as the stories of Hansel and Gretel, Sleeping Beauty and Snow White. These stories are all from Southern Germany and take place in German forests. To see the forests that inspired these stories, visit the Black Forest in south-west Germany.

The southern Black Forest

The most **remote** part of the Black Forest is in the south and borders on Switzerland and France. It is home to the highest mountains in the area.

A good place to start a journey is the Feldberg, the tallest mountain which is 1493 metres tall. You can see much of the Black Forest from the summit.

Another place that is popular with tourists is Lake Schluchsee. It is a huge lake fed by ancient **glaciers** and lots of people come here to swim in the summer.

Next, visit the nearby abbey, called Kloster Saint Trudpert. An abbey is a Christian religious settlement, and this one is about 1200 years old. It was built by Irish monks who wanted to spread Christianity to the area. Today it serves as a home for nuns. Monks and nuns are men and women who live away from society and serve God.

▼ THE BLACK FOREST

The Black Forest appears even more magical under the cover of fog. The tall, dark evergreens and high peaks look most dramatic at sunrise.

CYCLING IN THE BLACK FOREST ▶
This is just one of many activities taking place in the Black Forest region.

The central Black Forest

The city of Freiburg is often called the capital of the Black Forest. The first place to go in Freiburg is the Münster. This church is one of the most beautiful in Germany and building began in the year 1200. It is made from red stone with some colourful stained glass windows inside. They are almost 700 years old.

Next, go west to Freiburg's university. The buildings of the old university are very interesting. If you are hungry, try one of the local restaurants for a hearty German lunch. German sausages, cabbage and, of course, Black Forest gateau made with chocolate and cherries are specialities.

The northern Black Forest

The northern region of the Black Forest is a great place to take some photos. It is filled with dark valleys, ancient bridges and thick woodland. Walkers will find some of the best trails around the river Nagold and the river Murg.

One of the best ways to end a visit to the Black Forest is in Baden-Baden. This town has always been a favourite holiday spot for Europe's rich and famous. There are many health **spas** here and they are perfect for getting some rest and exercise before returning to the modern world. There are several beautiful gardens to explore and visitors can even have lessons at the famous golf course.

◀ IN FREIBURG

Walking around Freiburg is the best way to experience its charm. These buildings look like life-size gingerbread houses.

LICHEN ▶

Lichen are tiny plants that grow on the sides of rocks and trees. You can see many different colours and varieties of lichen in the Black Forest.

Holidays

Germans celebrate more public holidays than most other countries in Europe. German Unity Day is 3 October. It is a national holiday that celebrates Germany's **reunification** in 1990. There are also regional festivals such as the Oktoberfest in Munich Many of the major public holidays in Germany are Christian festivals. Christmas, celebrating the birth of Jesus, is one of the most important. Easter is also an important festival for Germans. Easter **commemorates** the death and resurrection of Jesus.

▲ MIME ARTISTS
Three mime artists wear the German colours at a German Unity Day celebration.

Learning the language

English	German	How to say it
Good day	Guten tag	GOO-ten TAHG
Good morning	Guten morgen	GOO-ten MOR-gun
Goodbye	Auf wiedersehen	OFF VEE-der-zay-en
Thank you	Danke schön	DAHN-keh SHOON
You're welcome	Bitte schön	BIH-teh SHOON
My name is _____	Ich heisse _____	EESH HI-seh____
I'm from _____	Ich komme aus	EESH KOM-meh OWS

Quick facts

Germany

Capital
Berlin

Borders
Denmark, Baltic Sea, North
Sea (N)
Poland, Czech Republic (E)
Austria, Switzerland (S)
France, Luxembourg,
Belgium, Netherlands (W)

Area
356,973 sq km
(137,828 sq miles)

Population
83,251,851

▼ Main religious groups

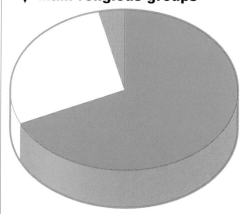

Largest cities
Berlin (3,477,900 people)
Hamburg (1,703,800)
Munich (1,251,100)
Cologne (963,300)
Frankfurt (656,200)

■ Christian 68%
☐ Other or unaffiliated 28.3%
■ Muslim 3.7%

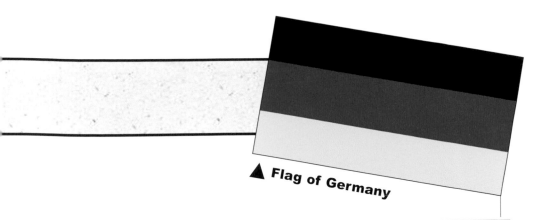

▲ Flag of Germany

Coastline
2389 km (1484 miles)

Longest river ▶
Rhine 1320 km (820 miles)

Literacy rate
99% of people in Germany
can read and write

Major industries
iron and steel, cement,
chemicals, machinery, vehicles,
machine tools, electronics, food
and beverages, shipbuilding,
textiles

Main crops and livestock
Wheat, barley, rye, potatoes, sugar
beet, fruit, cattle, pigs, poultry

Natural resources
Iron ore, coal, potash,
timber, lignite, uranium,
copper, natural gas,
salt, nickel

◀ **Monetary unit**
Euro

43

People to know

◀ Anne Frank

Anne Frank was a German Jew born in 1929. When the Nazis came to power, she and her family went into hiding in the Netherlands. Eventually, Anne was found and sent to a death camp where she died. While in hiding, Anne kept a diary. Today this diary has been read by millions all over the world.

Gerhard Schroeder ▶

Gerhard Schroeder did not start out thinking he would be a famous politician. In fact, he wanted to be a salesman. After joining the Social Democratic Party, though, he became interested in politics. In 1998, he became chancellor of Germany.

◀ Steffi Graf

Steffi Graf was born in 1969. She became a famous tennis player when she was just a teenager, winning all four of the world's major tournaments in 1988. She went on to win them several more times. Over the years, she has won more than 20 million dollars in prize money.

Do you want to know more about Germany? Have a look at the books below.

Take your camera to: Germany, Ted Park
  (Raintree, 2003)
A guide to famous places, cities and festivals in Germany, this book shows you where to go and what to photograph.

Nations of the World: Germany, Greg Nickles and Niki Walker. (Raintree, 2003)
This book explores German history and culture in detail, and examines the geography, economy and lifestyle of the country.

Turning Points in History: The Fall of the Berlin Wall – The Cold War Ends, Nigel Kelly.
  (Heinemann Library, 2000)
Learn about the key events and the cause and effect of the Fall of the Berlin Wall. Discover what made this an important turning point in history.

Heinemann Profiles: Adolf Hitler and *Anne Frank,* Richard Tames. (Heinemann Library, 1998)
These two books explore the lives of these very different Germans, and their contribution to the twentieth century.

Glossary

architecture style or design used in a building

brewer person who makes beer

chancellor title of the leader of Germany

Cold War conflict between the USA and the Soviet Union that stopped short of armed warfare

commemorate do something special to honour someone or something

communist type of government in which the state owns all the industry and assigns jobs to the people

culture way of life of a society or civilization

death camp Nazi prison camp where Jews and other prisoners were taken to be killed

democracy government with leaders who are elected by the people

docks landing areas where ships load and unload cargo or stay for repairs

dynasty series of rulers from the same family

economic depression time when businesses do badly and people cannot make any money

enchanted thing or place that seems magical

fertile good for growing crops

founded to have started or set up something

glacier large sheet of ice found near the North and South Poles

Holocaust murder of 6 million Jews by the Nazis during World War II

invade enter another country by force